A Journal
of
God's Breath

A Path of Intentions

by **Ricky Manna**

A Journal of God's Breath – A Path of Intentions

Copyright © 2016 by Ricky Manna Books Ltd.

Welland, Ontario, Canada

First Createspace printing January 2017

ISBN Canada: 978-0-9951679-0-2

ISBN-13: 978-1532734083

ISBN-10:1532734085

Dedication

I want to dedicate this book exclusively to the Holy Spirit. I believe the Holy Spirit (sometimes called God's messenger) has led me powerfully when I share my story to others simply by asking for guidance when speaking.

This page is intentionally blank

Table of Contents

Introduction

Congratulations on getting this personal journal. Whether it is for yourself or a friend I am positive it will become a landmark in your spiritual journey.

I am going to go as far as *promise you* that your relationship with God, no matter what level of faith you are at, will grow in a real way as your progress through this daily personal journal for the next 365 days. You will encounter spiritual experience.

What I am going to do is, I am going to propose a unique idea for you to consider. Then I want you to combine it with a **spiritual intention** for that week. A spiritual intention is a desire and commitment in thought (and spirit) to move towards an idea for revelation. We are opening ourselves to a spiritual idea and asking God to teach us what He wants us to experience in this particular area. It is an opportunity to increase our fellowship with Him and grow stronger in our faith. It's also important that you know you can enjoy this path. Even though you may (and probably will) come into deep realizations because of this, you can really enjoy your interaction with God as you walk with Him with the provided intention for that week. Even if the walk becomes difficult, your relationship with Him will deepen significantly.

First, what I am going to ask of you is to use an open mind and consider that the wind is actually God's breath. I want you to consider it (and feel it) as God telling you that He just gave you a **"hey you"** moment. The process I will lay out for you will actually be a form of meditation by using an intention for a week. If you wish to use one of the intentions I give you for a longer period than one week feel free to do so.

If you have never meditated before you will find this method of meditating a lot of fun.

Meditation can be compared very closely to eating. Imagine you have an apple in your hand in front of you. If your name is Adam, please forgive me. It *will* work out this time.

When you look at the apple and you are considering taking a bite of it. That can be the same as considering a spiritual concept or idea. At this moment you are deciding if you wish to move forward by biting into the apple. Comparatively, by meditating, you are considering whether to allow the idea or concept into your mind.

The next step is to physically take a bite out of the apple which can be compared to *allowing* the idea or concept into your mind to consider. Then chewing on the apple as you roll it around in your mouth is the same as thinking about how the idea relates or applies to you and your life in the different ways it may help you.

Then when you have chewed the apple enough so it will go down easily, you swallow the masticated or chewed up apple. Comparatively, when you have pondered the spiritual idea or concept in enough ways and are willing to accept it, you accept it by allowing it into your spirit.

The cool part is at this time the food nourishes your body while the idea has nourished your spirit! They both become part of your growth.

If you believe God made all things it shouldn't be a big stretch for you to consider His breath upon you as a possibility.

The premise of an open mind is that you don't have to give up a particular belief or opinion, just be willing **to consider the possibility** of a given idea. That's it. You are not giving anything up, you still have your original beliefs intact. Maintaining an open mind can prove to be one of the greatest assets we have. This principle has led me personally to many exciting spiritual discoveries that strengthened my faith in amazing ways which in turn helped me when I needed it most.

Next is another concept or idea I want you to consider. It is my belief that when God said "Let there be light" He didn't just create light out of nothing, although he could have if He wanted to. He actually **became** light! When He said "Let there be water" again, He **became** water. I believe He did this to show us the power He gave to the spoken word. He made all of creation from words. I am sure your mind is ringing right now with whom the Word *became* as well! When this was taught to me I meditated on it for a couple days and as a result of this I had the most powerful spiritual experience of my life. I felt the presence of God and "walked with Christ" for 3 or 4 days. I will never forget it.

Time and time again He emphasizes the proper use of words to us and how to use them. Take some time to research this idea in His Word when you can.

For example, He said we are to speak (and even pray) BOLDLY, and even with CONFIDENCE. So pay attention to the words you use, especially in prayer.

Getting back to God's existence, God certainly *could have* just snapped His fingers and created each thing out of nothing, but He chose *to become* what He created.

As his children we were then given this power of creation to create with our own words. With the words we choose we can create harmony or disharmony. Love, or hatred. Happiness or pain and resentment. This power of creation has been passed along to us just as He said "As you say, so shall it be".(NUMBERS 14:28) and (PROVERBS 6:2) "You are taken by the words of your mouth". Which way do you want your words to take you? For good or destruction? Your choice.

Even psychologists' today state that our own words can limit or empower us in very significant ways. The word "can't" is one of the most powerful words in our vocabulary. When we use this word against ourselves it has a crippling effect. For example, if you say "I can't remember names" guess what? You won't be able to! The more you repeat this phrase against yourself the worse it will get.

However your (spoken) words can heal you as well. Just by acknowledging a difficulty, (truth) and being willing to try, (healing and faith) we can turn around any limitation we impose on ourselves. The results will be amazing. Words are very, very powerful.

I experienced this principle first hand when I was in Grade 12. It was my last year of high school and I needed all my credits or I would have to do the entire year over. It was a very difficult time for me and I did not believe I would be willing to do another year in that school if I did not pass that year.

If I failed any of my courses, it would prevent me from graduating and getting a diploma.

Fortunately I was doing well enough in school with all of my courses except one. It was mathematics. My scores averaged around 38 and a final average score of 55 for the year was required to pass. It seemed no matter what I did, I just couldn't raise my scores. I kept saying to people that I couldn't do math. Math and I were strangers that made no sense to each other. I'm sure I used the word "can't" in many contexts showing how incapable I believed I was when it came to this strange strategy called mathematics.

When I realized that I had to find a way to pass math or I would not get my diploma, I panicked. "*What can I do*?" I thought.

I remember going to the school library and in desperation I told the school librarian of my dilemma. "I have just the book for you" she said, and handed me this paperback novel. The book was called **Psycho-Cybernetics** by Maxwell Maltz.

What I gleaned from the book was to stop saying the word "can't". That the word was actually programming my mind and that I would be totally unable to do whatever I used that word on. I was literally programming my mind to cripple itself! There were other awesome concepts in this book but this is the one that stood out for me at the time.

Fortunately the book also outlined the healing process to reverse the damage, which I utilized immediately. I simply needed to be honest and express if I had difficulty (with whatever issue) and that I would try. More importantly, to also verbally acknowledge any improvement I experienced.

Guess what? I passed. Not by a lot but for the first time in a couple years my scores rose high enough to give me the passing mark I needed and I went home with my diploma. Today I pay close attention anytime that word escapes my lips. I even raised my son using that principle. My son was not even allowed to say the word "can't" in a sentence. To say that a problem he was facing was difficult and he was having trouble with it was fine but it was imperative to leave the door open for the brain (and spirit) to use its ability to function in this area without programming him to fail. You may think this was extreme or even weird for me to insist this upon my son but it had some very positive effects on him as he grew up.

He even found ways to have fun with it. One day when I caught him using "can't" he looked to me and said "I can't believe I forgot".

The point of all of this is that our words have an *inherited* power. A God given power to use words creatively or destructively. It's up to us.

Getting back to paying attention to God's breath, I want you to be safe. If you're walking across the street and have a gust of wind or mild breeze hit you, I don't want you to stop in the middle of the street! I still want you to be aware of your surroundings.

So when you get to a safer location you can make a note of these things. What I want you to do is list the things that were going on when the breeze hit you. See how the any of the questions relate to the intention you chose for that week that are listed on page 119.

I will place a these special questions at the back of the journal so they will be easy to reference each day if you need to look them over again.

This will take practice but your spiritual awareness will grow quite steadily as you progress with your journal each day.

At the end of the day, and this is very important, I ask that you find something to **speak** gratitude about. Most days will be easy to find something to be grateful for. However, there will be a day (or more) that you will have to work hard to find something to be genuinely grateful for. It's just the way it is, not all days will be great. I encourage you to speak genuine words of gratitude for what happened that day. **This is a critical part of the process so make sure each day is ended this way.**

This is actually a lesson and experience on meditation as you will be contemplating a powerful spiritual principle with the *intention* of knowing God better. Not only that, I promise you that you will have powerful spiritual experiences and greater spiritual understandings as a result.

Feel free to add to your list of things to ask yourself, or contemplate when the breeze or wind touches you. Or even other intentions you would like to have. I would love to hear from you about what other ideas you come up with. I may even add them to the next book with a reference to who suggested them. Or if you prefer to be anonymous that is fine too.

Alright! Are you ready for a new adventure? Begin your week with the intention for that week and at the time that works for you, apply the questions about God's breath that day. If there wasn't any time that you can think of where God's Breath was there in your day, continue without it. It will happen, just be open and ready for it when it does happen. You could even get a small hand held device to record your thoughts until you can add them into your journal. It will be important however, for you to write down your thoughts and discoveries each day so you can see how your journey progresses. It doesn't matter if it goes slowly or quickly. It will be your path that He chooses for you, so enjoy it.

IMPORTANT

I have created a special intention for you to use when you feel you need a rest. Believe me when I say this can be quite the spiritual ride so you might be tempted to put this process aside for a while. I encourage you not to! Use intention #23 to rest yourself and when you are ready (even if it needs to be longer than a week) start on the next intention.

Are you ready? Then let's get started!

A List of Intentions:

Try to keep notes each day for the intention you are focusing on. Not only will it help you keep your attention on what you are doing, it will show you the discoveries you have had when you look back at this journal in the future.

Week 1

Think and feel appreciation this week. Refuse to entertain any thoughts of doubt or worry. Find a way to be appreciative for *all* things. Even when you think things are going wrong.

_____

_____

_____

_____

_____

_____

_____

_____

_____

_____

_____

_____

_____

_____

_____

_____

_____

_____

_____

Week 2

Realize that every thought you entertain impacts you. When you can realize what thoughts are being entertained in your mind you may have more insight to the types of thoughts that follow them, and maybe even rule your day.

God may send a breeze your way to help you 'wake up' in that moment.

_____
_____
_____
_____
_____
_____
_____
_____
_____
_____
_____
_____
_____
_____
_____
_____
_____
_____
_____
_____
_____
_____
_____
_____
_____
_____
_____
_____
_____

Week 3

Use this week as a limitless well of forgiveness. When you see acts of weakness from others, (like anger, impatience or even violence) extend thoughts from your own spirit of forgiveness. Extend this form of Godly love even to yourself. See and feel yourself as God does. Perfect. Once you have done this, embrace yourself as you are. Do this because He does. He loves you just as you are, right at this moment. I encourage you to find a definition of the word embrace that resonates with you.

_____

_____

_____

_____

_____

_____

_____

_____

_____

_____

_____

_____

_____

_____

_____

_____

_____

_____

_____

_____

_____

Week 4

Let go of needing love from others, even family and loved ones. Human love is conditional. When we anger or disappoint the people we love they sometimes say or do things that hurt us deeply. We cannot afford this kind of conditional love in our life. We need perfect, unrelenting love. Only God is capable of this kind of love. Instead *give love* to those around you. You can do this through words of encouragement, humor, or even just listening.

Remember that it is by giving that we receive. Actively seek God's perfect love, ask for it, embrace it and allow it to fill you up. It is the only type of love you truly need. Unrelenting Agape (unconditional) love. This will provide you with all the self-esteem that you need. You are a child of God. The Creator of all things, and He loves you every moment of every day. Nothing you can do will lessen the amount of love He has for you! Seek this love only and you will fill up with agape love to give to others.

_____

_____

_____

_____

_____

_____

_____

_____

_____

_____

_____

_____

_____

_____

_____

_____

_____

_____

_____

Week 5

Watch for thoughts of self-importance. These are ways of how we compare ourselves against others, even those we consider sinners or lost souls. These thoughts bring us out of harmony as they are judgmental and separate us from God and his children. Disgust, envy and even jealousy can be emotions that our judgements are hiding in. Be Christ like in these thoughts of others and yourself.

_____

_____

_____

_____

_____

_____

_____

_____

_____

_____

_____

_____

_____

_____

_____

_____

_____

_____

_____

_____

_____

_____

_____

_____

_____

_____

_____

_____

Week 6

Step on your ego this week! Look for thoughts of what you consider others may be thinking of you. Are you worried that some people hold the wrong opinion of you? That is your ego peeking out. Let go of it!

_____

_____

_____

_____

_____

_____

_____

_____

_____

_____

_____

_____

_____

_____

_____

_____

_____

_____

_____

_____

_____

_____

_____

_____

_____

_____

Week 7

Make this a week of surrender. Find things in your life you can surrender to God. Your love of others, your desire to be what you think you should be, etc. Invite God's perfection into your weaknesses by surrendering each self-effort you are using this week. This can be an intention you can utilize for a longer period as it may take some time to see all the ways you are trying to do things. Ask God to help you see what needs to be surrendered. By doing this you bring His strength into these areas of your life. It will change things significantly!

_____

_____

_____

_____

_____

_____

_____

_____

_____

_____

_____

_____

_____

_____

_____

_____

_____

_____

_____

_____

_____

_____

Week 8

At your core, I want you to place the knowledge and belief that if you were the only person on earth, Jesus still would have given his life to save you. He loves you that much. Allow that to filter into the deepest parts of your heart, mind, and spirit.

_____

_____

_____

_____

_____

_____

_____

_____

_____

_____

_____

_____

_____

_____

_____

_____

_____

_____

_____

_____

_____

_____

_____

_____

_____

Week 9

Now let's take that act of love even deeper. I want you to know that God the Father loves you as much as He loves Jesus. God loved us as His children even though we were lost. Then He commanded Jesus to give His life for us so we would be reconciled by His sacrifice. So as His children we are loved deeply. So much so that His only begotten Son was given to sacrifice his blood for us as the final sacrificing of the Lamb. So as a child of God you are worthy! Not by what we do but by **what** we are, His children! Before the sacrifice He loved you so much that He sent His own Son to pay the cost that was ours to pay. So He paid a debt that wasn't even His!

_____

_____

_____

_____

_____

_____

_____

_____

_____

_____

_____

_____

_____

_____

_____

_____

_____

_____

_____

_____

_____

_____

_____

Week 10

Find a reason to be grateful for *all* situations, no matter what they are. It's easy to be grateful when things are going our way, but the challenge is to be grateful when things are not going our way. Doing this will launch your spiritual growth into the next level.

Let me give you an example:

Around ten years ago I was driving home from dropping my son off at his mother's house. It was a beautiful spring day and the relationship between my son's mother and I had been improving greatly over the prior 7 or so years. As I was driving home I began to speak words of gratitude. I said that I was grateful for the wonderful son I had been entrusted with, the improving relationship with his mother, and how beautiful the day was. I even spoke gratitude for the car I was driving. This car was put together by a friend 5 years before then and I was given the car for $500. The car worked like a charm and by now it had around 200 thousand miles on it. At that point I literally said out loud: "Dad (I call him Dad because He is my true Father) even if this car were to break down right now, I would still be grateful". Guess what happened? Yup, that's right, the car died 30 seconds after I verbalized my gratitude. Normally you might think a person would start complaining, saying this wasn't fair, but I didn't. I literally got out of the car (after it coasted to the side of the road) laughing my face off. I thought it was hilarious. I saw it that way because I see and know my Lord Father as my supply. I know that as long as remain faithful and do the work He sends me, it is His job to take care of me and my family. So I'm walking down the highway laughing saying "Ok Dad, you have to get me another car because I have a job I have to get to. So I'm looking forward to seeing you getting it done"! Within 10 minutes I noticed a familiar truck approaching me on the highway. It was a young man I was mentoring at the time along with his girlfriend beside him. He pulled over and asked what I was doing walking on the highway and I answered that my car has died a half mile back. So he offered me a ride back home. While we were driving back he mentioned that he had been unable to get out of town for the last two hours. Something kept coming up which prevented him from leaving until a few minutes before he found me on the highway. I just said to him that he couldn't leave town yet because I needed a ride home from the highway and Dad chose him to be my ride. At first when he heard this he was a little unsure about what I was saying but later when the whole story unfolded he knew it was true.

Once I arrived home I called the fellow who put the car together for me (I was mentoring him as well) and asked if he had time to look over the car to see what happened. He said yes, and we went out to where the car was to look it over. Unfortunately he couldn't see what the problem was and he towed it to a nearby gas station where a friend of his worked, to see what the problem was.

So I went to work with a co-worker the next day and later called the mechanic to see if he knew what the problem was. He did, it was the timing belt. For this car however it was over a thousand dollars installed which was more than the value of the car. I asked him how much he wanted for the work he had done (taking the engine apart) and he said there was no charge. I had no money at all (like most of us I was living check to check) so I told him to keep the car for his effort.

I felt a short jolt of anxiety when I said that but I turned it over again to Dad to resolve the problem as He promises in the Bible.

So now I waited, all the while fighting any thoughts or feelings of worry or anxiety with God's word. A few hours later a fellow sitting next to me said he was looking at an ad for a car dealership that was offering used cars with no loans being turned down. I told him that I had had two bankruptcies already and that I was sure I wouldn't get approved. He just looked at me (with a bit of a frown) and re-instated that they said "no loans not approved"! I know from previous experiences when God is knocking so I meekly said I would check it out. My sister drove me there and an awesome looking Chevy had just arrived for me to look over. It was a beautiful car and ran smoother than my old car by a long shot. I applied for the loan and guess what? Again God came through. Not only that, my work on the Internet began to improve and the money needed to pay for the loan was there so I wouldn't have to use any of my paycheck for it. So God came through bigtime, and in three days I was driving a second hand car that looked brand new.

There is more to the story that happened a few months afterwards but this demonstrates giving gratitude and standing by your words. When I lost this job a few years later I voiced my gratitude for having a good job for the last 16 years. Every time I felt worry about how I was going to pay the bills I fought them back and relied on His promise to be there for me, which He has. Every time.

So do the same, speak gratitude in times of difficulty. Stand on His promises and verbalize you are depending on Him. Then get ready and watch for His glory!

Week 11

Spend more time listening today than speaking. Keep the conversation on topic and ask questions to show interest in what the person has to say. Don't use the conversation to relate a story of your own unless you keep it very brief and then make a statement that will bring the conversation back to their topic. This is known as "I Thou". It is an excellent way to give a person time to be heard. Many people wish to be loved but few are willing to give love by listening. Be the exception to the rule.

_____

_____

_____

_____

_____

_____

_____

_____

_____

_____

_____

_____

_____

_____

_____

_____

_____

_____

_____

_____

_____

_____

_____

Week 12

Give a total stranger a word of kindness. It can be as simple as "Good morning" or better yet, just "Morning" sometimes people have a quick answer like "What's so good about it?" So just say "morning," it's safer.

I want to let you in on how powerful this can be. A gentleman by the name of Edward Lorenz was given numerous awards for his work with the "Butterfly Effect". It basically refers to a concept that small things can lead to large effects, even globally. Now imagine small things empowered with God's Agape love! How much more powerful would that be? More than once I have seen surprise on a stranger's face once I said "Morning" to them with a small smile. They sometimes weren't even looking my way when I said it. Perhaps our acts of kindness (imbued with God's power) will cause them to re-evaluate their day. Maybe even pass along some kindness to another! This is only one example. Ask God to show you other simple ways to help others with simple acts of kindness. Remember that their response to you does not matter, only your act of kindness matters. If they tell you to go fish, that's fine. You're not offering conditional kindness. Keep smiling!

_____

_____

_____

_____

_____

_____

_____

_____

_____

_____

_____

_____

_____

_____

Week 13

Voice gratitude for those who anger you! They have exposed a weakness (or a button) that you have. Now you can surrender this button to God! He will replace your weakness with His strength! The same with embarrassment or envy. Anything that disturbs your happiness or peace can be surrendered for a new source of strength. Then speak words of gratitude and forgiveness towards these people. It really works, just keep at it!

_____

_____

_____

_____

_____

_____

_____

_____

_____

_____

_____

_____

_____

_____

_____

_____

_____

_____

_____

_____

Week 14

Keep an eye out for people or things showing up to help you. It could be with a simple question you have or help with something important. All you have to do is ask. I was given the blessing of being mentored by an amazing Native Canadian man who was deeply spiritual and taught me many tremendous lessons on life, God and human nature. At one point in my path with him it was time for me to learn more about God. So he told me to ask God to show me more about Him so I could know Him better. I asked this in sincerity and then let it go.

A few days later a lady walked up to me and said "Ricky, you've got to read this book. It's really good". She knew nothing about the path I was on at the time. I thanked her for taking the time to show it to me but I was busy with some work my mentor had given me (duh),lol. Then a couple days after that a different person approached me and he had the same book in his hand. "Hey man' you should read this book, it's pretty cool". I said that someone had already mentioned it to me but I was working with my mentor at the time and I needed to focus on that. I thanked him and he left.

On my honor, another person walked up to me a day or so later holding the same book. "Ricky, have you heard about this book"? All of a sudden I realized what was happening. God wasn't knocking at my door, He was pounding! I sheepishly took the book and thanked him for bringing it to my attention. Later after I read it I discovered the book was based on a true story of a child living in England who had an extraordinary relationship with God. The book was called **Mr. God, This is Anna.** After reading this book I entered into a deeper understanding of God that helped me tremendously. I urge you to read it. (knock, knock!)

Week 15

Use your emotions as flags that show you are off your spiritual track. To me, the most significant one that shows me I am off track is worry. If you think about it, worry is actually self-reliance. When I worry it is usually because I am concerned how *I* am going to fix or resolve a particular issue. The more severe the situation, the more powerful the emotion can be. Our emotions are a big part of who and what we are.

One of the worst things we do to ourselves is deny our feelings by saying it is wrong for us to feel a certain way. What I am talking about are the emotions that seem to come out of nowhere and make no sense to us. They can be all sorts of emotions. Fear, anxiety, remorse and a host of others. Even though we don't understand why we feel this way it is critical to never say that it is wrong to feel this way. Our feeling are real, but they are not always based on reality. The important thing is to accept this feeling like it's a troubled child. Accept it and allow it a place to live, but not a position of control. Just a home. You are feeling this way for a reason and working with the emotion later may lead to some stark discoveries. Then seeing the emotion as it is, invite God to resolve the issue as you examine this "troubled child'. You may find your emotional nature becoming calmer as a result of nurturing these feelings.

_____
_____
_____
_____
_____
_____
_____
_____
_____
_____
_____
_____
_____
_____

Week 16

As one of God's kids your nature is joy! Look up the word "joy" and find a definition that resonates with you. One definition I found that resonates with me was: "have the heart of a child"! Spend your week seeking this nature from within. This will be very cool, just wait…

_____
_____
_____
_____
_____
_____
_____
_____
_____
_____
_____
_____
_____
_____
_____
_____
_____
_____
_____
_____
_____
_____
_____
_____
_____
_____
_____
_____

Week 17

Be like a baby. This is building on the joy nature. A child has no teeth, no hair and flatulence. Yet they are totally happy. When they have a need they let us know of course, but how soon do they return to joy? Even in sleep the wonder of God's beauty is on their faces. Spend some time watching a baby if you are able. See the beauty of God's kingdom on their face. Maybe it is because it wasn't long ago that they were in His company?

_____
_____
_____
_____
_____
_____
_____
_____
_____
_____
_____
_____
_____
_____
_____
_____
_____
_____
_____
_____

Week 18

How are your perceptions today? Do you see the world in strife or harmony? Sure there is evidence showing much turmoil, but what else? Do you see only the bad, or are you seeing people working together? Open your perception to seeing more by asking for your eyes and ears to be opened. As a last resort *you* can be the change you wish upon the world.

_____

_____

_____

_____

_____

_____

_____

_____

_____

_____

_____

_____

_____

_____

_____

_____

_____

_____

_____

_____

_____

_____

_____

_____

Week 19

Treat everything that jars you out of your routine as a possible blessing. Maybe a breath of fresh air is being brought to you to show you another perspective. Try to avoid resenting the change. Find a way to open yourself to it. Perhaps it's a big change you are facing. Make a prayer of sincere gratitude to bring peace and understanding about it. Express real gratitude to make it easier to face. Be like a baby, they love change. When you see other problems surfacing, take responsibility. Even though it may seem that you have no involvement in the issue look hard to see if you had had something to do with it in the past. We're not looking for blame, just accountability. Many times what is being attracted to us is reflecting what is going on inside of us. Feel free to work on this one for longer if needed

_____

_____

_____

_____

_____

_____

_____

_____

_____

_____

_____

_____

_____

_____

_____

_____

_____

_____

_____

Week 20

Let go of the need to always show people where they are going wrong. Instead support them in their decisions (as long as it is not dangerous) and help them to see consequences that may happen as a result. God in interested in all His children, even the lost ones. Be quick to defend God though if they blame Him for their issues. If they don't believe in God, why then are they blaming Him? In kindness you can help them to see where their own decisions could have been the culprit. There are two powerful movers in this world. The power of God, and the power of example. Both move mountains. (also known as blockheads... I was one)

_____
_____
_____
_____
_____
_____
_____
_____
_____
_____
_____
_____
_____
_____
_____
_____
_____
_____
_____
_____

Week 21

Focus on new ways on how to be kinder to your closest relative. YOU. Speak words of kindness and encouragement. Speak out loud against negative thoughts or feeling that may surface using self-talk and scripture to cast out these thoughts. God **never** sends messages of guilt or shame, so cast these out with His blood.

_____

_____

_____

_____

_____

_____

_____

_____

_____

_____

_____

_____

_____

_____

_____

_____

_____

_____

_____

_____

_____

_____

Week 22

REST INTENTION

This is the intention I spoke of should you feel that you need to rest and just fathom all that has happened for you. It is very important that you stay on this path so don't decide to just stop your journey for a while. You can take a break by simply resting in Him!

The premise of this intention is that each day you will simply reside in His company. You are not looking for answers or posing any questions. You are simply holding hands and live beside Him. Should you feel burdened, refer to (and speak out loud) the scripture Matthew 11:30 "For my yoke is easy and my burden is light". Jesus will bear the load and our yoke becomes as light as air. This is a powerful promise that I have been given any time I surrendered a burden to Him. He took over the weight of it and I was free to move forward unhindered. I urge you to do the same with anything that is holding you back or slowing your progress. **Feel free to re-use this intention anytime you feel the need.**

_____
_____
_____
_____
_____
_____
_____
_____
_____
_____
_____
_____
_____
_____
_____

Week 23

Outward appearances are seldom inward reality. This saying has become a deeply seated truth for me once I began practicing it. How many times have we seen couples who appeared to have a great relationship when we later find out it is the exact opposite. Or that a service being offered is nowhere near what is being advertised? It's not a recommendation to be negative but to just start opening our eyes. Stop making judgements based on what we see, as "things may not be all that they seem". Sometimes our troubles are a blessing in disguise, while for another their abundance may be the source of their troubles. Prosperity can have more perils than poverty. Take a second look at your assessments of your world.

_____

_____

_____

_____

_____

_____

_____

_____

_____

_____

_____

_____

_____

_____

_____

_____

_____

_____

_____

Week 24

God does so much for us that we never know about. There are so many things that bring blessings together for us that we will not find out about until we are in His presence. I heard a person say once that God can see the goal posts at the end of the field while we can only see the next play. Contemplate His plan for you as He moves in mysterious ways. Be grateful for what you cannot see.

_____

_____

_____

_____

_____

_____

_____

_____

_____

_____

_____

_____

_____

_____

_____

_____

_____

_____

_____

_____

_____

_____

_____

Week 25

What is your identity based on? Is it the job you hold, the marriage you have, the possessions you own? Consider how quickly these things can fall away. Jobs are lost without warning. Downsizing takes good paying jobs away from capable people, sometimes along with their pension. Depending on our vehicle to perform flawlessly is sometimes a lesson we learn at the most inconvenient time. Where is your confidence placed? Living in faith, especially when times are really tough, is difficult. The thoughts of security and contentment can change quickly to utter turmoil when these things collapse. Use this time of stability to place your identity in God, not the world.

_____

_____

_____

_____

_____

_____

_____

_____

_____

_____

_____

_____

_____

_____

_____

_____

_____

_____

_____

_____

_____

Week 26

Prayer for the week. I found this prayer a few years ago and it continues to impress me as a prayer of selflessness and surrender.

"Lord, I offer myself to Thee. To build with me and do with me as thou wilt. Relieve me Lord of the bondage of self, that I may better do my will. Take away my difficulties that victory over them may bear witness to those I would help of Thy Power, Thy Love, and Thy way of life. May I do Thy will today and always".

So this asks that we be made better not for ourselves, but so those around us would see us being helped in powerful ways. This can convey hope to others by seeing God working in our lives. Use this prayer for the week and be open to what happens.

_____

_____

_____

_____

_____

_____

_____

_____

_____

_____

_____

_____

_____

_____

_____

_____

_____

_____

Week 27

Mountains out of molehills. We tend by nature to be negative thinkers. It's so easy to get hung up on small details and become unable to see the big picture. When a person does an injustice it becomes the only thing we can see about them. We forget the good they have done and see the imperfection. Watch for areas where this may be infecting your perception of others.

_____

_____

_____

_____

_____

_____

_____

_____

_____

_____

_____

_____

_____

_____

_____

_____

_____

_____

_____

_____

_____

_____

_____

_____

_____

_____

Week 28

God thinks you're great!

Having a hard day at work or at home? Are your co-workers angry with you, or maybe a family member at home? It's difficult to be steadfast when it's easier to give in to keep the peace. As long as we are doing what we believe is right, and operating out of love, you're doing just great. Give it some time and have a heart to heart talk with the person affected when the time presents itself.

_____

_____

_____

_____

_____

_____

_____

_____

_____

_____

_____

_____

_____

_____

_____

_____

_____

_____

_____

_____

_____

_____

Week 29

Seek His presence. Nothing can stop a believer who feels the presence of God in their lives. Uncertainty will melt away like the morning dew with the rising of the Son. The sun too! Fear will be like ice on the summer ocean, no matter how big it is, it will subside. Let your fear of any obstacle retreat of the presence of your belief in His power!

_____

_____

_____

_____

_____

_____

_____

_____

_____

_____

_____

_____

_____

_____

_____

_____

_____

_____

_____

_____

_____

_____

_____

_____

_____

Week 30

Use this week to examine your dependencies. Where have you placed your faith? This is simply an exercise that can help you to see where you may have placed people places or things ahead of God. I was quite an interesting learning experience for me, perhaps it will be for you as well. Don't use it as a reason to get down on yourself, simply surrender places where you have found your faith in places that can let you down. Let it bring you closer to Him.

_____

_____

_____

_____

_____

_____

_____

_____

_____

_____

_____

_____

_____

_____

_____

_____

_____

_____

_____

_____

_____

_____

_____

Week 31

Remember that it is in serving others that we will find our destiny. Not only that, you will find your gifts from Him. Everyone has them, no exceptions. Even though it may be hard to find them, open yourself to serving others in a Godly way and listen to the words of others. They may tell you what they believe are your gifts.

_____

_____

_____

_____

_____

_____

_____

_____

_____

_____

_____

_____

_____

_____

_____

_____

_____

_____

_____

_____

_____

_____

_____

_____

_____

_____

_____

Week 32

Make this a week of going over the understanding that God truly is all things. He is air, sunshine, earth and water. As you walk, wherever you are, keep in mind you are breathing Him in. Walking on Him, and actually seeing Him in various forms about you.

Allow this to soak into your mind and spirit.

_____
_____
_____
_____
_____
_____
_____
_____
_____
_____
_____
_____
_____
_____
_____
_____
_____
_____
_____
_____
_____
_____
_____
_____
_____
_____

Week 33

If you have discovered what your gift is, stir it up! Place your words of gratitude and reverence upon it. Your name is on it, make use of it. Just pray on how to get it going! If you are not aware of how God has gifted you, ask someone who's opinion you trust.

_____

_____

_____

_____

_____

_____

_____

_____

_____

_____

_____

_____

_____

_____

_____

_____

_____

_____

_____

_____

_____

_____

_____

_____

Week 34

Eric Hoffer said: "When people are free to do as they please, they usually imitate each other." The human being is the only creation that refuses to be what they are. Children of Almighty God! Don't be awestruck by other people and copy them. You are a specialist with special gifts, you were not created to be all things to all people. Take the difficult path and allow your uniqueness to flower.

_____
_____
_____
_____
_____
_____
_____
_____
_____
_____
_____
_____
_____
_____
_____
_____
_____
_____
_____
_____
_____
_____
_____

Week 35

Jesus died for us because he was passionate about all of us. What are you passionate about? Your true potential lies in what you are passionate about. If you add belief to your passion you will find conviction. What you passionately love is a clue to the gift you contain. Live this week with your passion.

_____

_____

_____

_____

_____

_____

_____

_____

_____

_____

_____

_____

_____

_____

_____

_____

_____

_____

_____

_____

_____

_____

_____

Week 36

If it was against the law to talk about God, would there be enough evidence to arrest you? You don't have to run around like a mad person trying to save souls, but do you talk about God as your best friend? Is He the Source of all things to you? Think about the last time you spoke about Him to another person. How long has it been? Perhaps there is room for improvement.

_____
_____
_____
_____
_____
_____
_____
_____
_____
_____
_____
_____
_____
_____
_____
_____
_____
_____
_____
_____
_____

Week 37

Has the "fear" emotion been showing itself lately? Fear wants to rob you of faith because it believes that it can convince you that what you cannot see will happen! Fear is a darkroom where negatives are developed. Turn the Light on! Burn those negatives out of yourself. Psalms 27:1 and 56:4 have some direction for us. So this week, feed your faith and watch your doubts starve to death.

_____

_____

_____

_____

_____

_____

_____

_____

_____

_____

_____

_____

_____

_____

_____

_____

_____

_____

_____

_____

_____

_____

_____

Week 38

What have you set your heart on? Getting or giving? There's nothing wrong with wanting to achieve things but what you are setting your heart on will determine how you will spend your life. Think about this for the week. Make sure you aren't headed for a disaster.

_____
_____
_____
_____
_____
_____
_____
_____
_____
_____
_____
_____
_____
_____
_____
_____
_____
_____
_____
_____
_____
_____
_____
_____

Week 39

There's an interesting saying that goes: "You are like a teabag, not worth much until you've been in some hot water." So many of us hold onto the tragedies of the past without realizing that God can turn them into our greatest treasure. Years of serious abuse were in my past yet I share them openly (when my spirit leads me) to let others know there is not only survival from these nightmares but actual hope! Hope spells; **H**ow **O**ther **P**eople **E**scaped! Spread some hope around, there may be someone drowning.

_____
_____
_____
_____
_____
_____
_____
_____
_____
_____
_____
_____
_____
_____
_____
_____
_____
_____
_____
_____
_____
_____

Week 40

Are you open to learning? It is impossible for a person to learn what they think they already know. Listen to the words of another and consider their perspective. It may bring you to a deeper understanding that you can activate in your life. Remember that we typically see things not as they are, but as *we* are, according to our present perspective. Make use of the great life changer called an open mind.

_____

_____

_____

_____

_____

_____

_____

_____

_____

_____

_____

_____

_____

_____

_____

_____

_____

_____

_____

_____

_____

_____

Week 41.

Open yourself this week to God's creative mind. Whether it is for a nagging problem that keeps resurfacing or a whole new idea. Just open yourself to it by asking for guidance.

_____
_____
_____
_____
_____
_____
_____
_____
_____
_____
_____
_____
_____
_____
_____
_____
_____
_____
_____
_____
_____
_____
_____
_____
_____

Week 42

How long has it been since you had a startling revelation? Ask God to open your mind to a new way of seeing your surroundings. Or perhaps a new idea on how to serve. Once you find it, act on it.

_____

_____

_____

_____

_____

_____

_____

_____

_____

_____

_____

_____

_____

_____

_____

_____

_____

_____

_____

_____

_____

_____

_____

Week 43

Do you suffer from procrastination? Most people do, it's pretty common. However many of the reasons that hold us back are actually old tapes we allow to run in our head. Maybe in your past you've said to yourself "I'll never allow myself to be hurt again." Or "I'll never be like my father (or mother)." Then find ourselves doing the very things we promised never to do!

In the commandment "Honor thy father and thy mother" I was torn on how to follow it. My father left when I was very young and spent his life drinking alcohol until it killed him. I never had a fatherly presence in my life and had always felt a deep need to have one. One day while meditating on it I realized I could place great honor on my father. I could learn to **not** do the things he had done! I knew the injury of not having a strong male presence in my life. The actual need of having loving discipline was something I craved! To have a strong shoulder when needed. He wasn't able to provide those things (and more) because of his addiction. He was a victim and so was I. So I honored him by giving my own son all the things my father could not give to me. It was because he could not give me these things that I knew and felt the importance of them. I was finally able to give true honor to my father by giving what he couldn't and seeing the real value of these actions. So if you find difficulty in moving forward in any particular situation, examine your feelings, many times they expose old tapes that are holding you back. Not just procrastination!

_____

_____

_____

_____

_____

_____

_____

_____

Week 44

Don't wait until you have everything you think you need to get moving ahead. God wants you to start now! He loves showing His glory through the weak. He always has. Don't allow idleness to paralyze your initiative. Start walking in the direction of your faith and watch God move obstacles. In Ecclesiastes 11:4, "If you wait for perfect conditions you'll never get anything done." Stand for something and you won't fall for anything!

_____

_____

_____

_____

_____

_____

_____

_____

_____

_____

_____

_____

_____

_____

_____

_____

_____

_____

_____

_____

_____

_____

Week 45

Mark Twain said: "The worst loneliness is not to be comfortable with yourself." Do find it necessary to have the radio on in the car? Feel more comfortable when you're in the company of others? This is not unusual when you are not comfortable in your own skin. This has led many to changing their feelings with (and becoming addicted to) alcohol, drugs, medications, porn, sex, and more. One of the keys to releasing yourself from these chains is self-acceptance. This is not so you can continue with the behavior without guilt, but to begin to love yourself as God does. With unconditional agape love you will find that fear, anger, guilt and shame will be driven out. Self-honor will propel growth in you and give you a place of comfort to live within. You will become your best human company.

_____

_____

_____

_____

_____

_____

_____

_____

_____

_____

_____

_____

_____

_____

_____

_____

_____

_____

_____

Week 46

There is already greatness in you. It is not something that is just in your future. It is there right now! The Kingdom of God, His essence and His love all reside in you right now. Allow that to reveal itself to you this week. Repeat it to yourself each day this week.

_____
_____
_____
_____
_____
_____
_____
_____
_____
_____
_____
_____
_____
_____
_____
_____
_____
_____
_____
_____
_____
_____

Week 47

Are you ready for battle? The bible says to wear the armor of God against the enemy but don't forget about the enemy within. Some of your greatest battles will be waged within your own mind. Many times I verbally voiced my belief in God's word against my inner voices. Each day as I walked down the street I would whisper His promises and stand as a child of God against anything that said otherwise. It took time but I didn't waiver. The attacks have subsided but not totally. Old tapes from the past can come into play when old situations resurface. Get used to standing on God's word and verbally refuse anything other than His truth. It's a great way to strengthen yourself for battle. Fight the good fight!

_____

_____

_____

_____

_____

_____

_____

_____

_____

_____

_____

_____

_____

_____

_____

_____

_____

_____

Week 48

  Are you wondering why things are not happening for you as you believe they should? Consider that your faith may be what is holding you back. Matthew 9:29 "According to your faith let it be to you." Perhaps your faith is not as full as needed for this miracle to happen. Is your faith stronger in things of this world than the next? Ask God to reveal your areas of faith that need to be strengthened.

_____

_____

_____

_____

_____

_____

_____

_____

_____

_____

_____

_____

_____

_____

_____

_____

_____

_____

_____

_____

_____

_____

_____

_____

_____

Week 49

What are you waiting for? Chances are you've been sitting on something that you know needs to be done but you kept putting it off. Start now! You can never be too soon doing the right thing because you will never know when it will be too late. Trying times are no time to quit trying. Just be faithful and get going. When faithfulness is most difficult it becomes the most necessary.

_____

_____

_____

_____

_____

_____

_____

_____

_____

_____

_____

_____

_____

_____

_____

_____

_____

_____

_____

_____

_____

Week 50

Do you have a forgiving heart? Look to Matthew 6: 14,15. If you forgive man for their transgressions, your heavenly Father will also forgive you. But if you do not forgive men then your Father will not forgive your transgressions." In in the prayer "Our Father" we enter into a contract of forgiveness when we say "Forgive us *as we forgive* those who trespass against us." Being "Christ like" is a duty as one of His followers. Leave the judgement up to Him, we can't handle it.

_____
_____
_____
_____
_____
_____
_____
_____
_____
_____
_____
_____
_____
_____
_____
_____
_____
_____
_____

Week 51

Be a brother or sister to everyone. That is who they truly are, family. Even unbelievers. The only difference between you and them is you have chosen to accept the price paid for you. The warrant has been lifted. Your accountability is no more. You should have tons of love in your heart just because of that! Now love another as yourself, forgiven and worthy to enter the kingdom. As a child of God your worth was shouted out by the heavens because His Son paid your price. Give a word of peace and understanding to another. Don't be a carpet, be a road sign!

Week 52

You've made it! Congratulations. I am very excited for you because you have made a real effort to become a living, loving, joyous, child of God. This week is for gratitude. Speak it openly and speak it privately between you and your Father. Share your gifts and boldly go where few people have gone before, in faith! You can leave your testimony where you purchased this journal to pave the way for others who are seeking Him. I am truly privileged to share in this wonderful path you have chosen. I look forward to meeting you in the Great Reality.

Use the next page for questions regarding God's breath.

God Bless

Rick Manna

Optional questions you can ask yourself regarding God's Breath today:

1. Where were you when a breeze was felt?

2. What were you doing?

3. What kind of breath (wind) was it? A subtle single breeze or a light wind that trickled across your entire face and body? Was it a sudden gust or a strong wind you had to brace against?

4. What were you thinking about just before it happened? This will take practice to become more aware of your thoughts.

5. What were you feeling before you felt the breeze? Anger, fear, happiness, joy.

6. Where were you going at the time?

7. After you felt His breath, what occurred to you at that moment, or even later that day? Did you feel differently? More peaceful, or motivated, or even disturbed? Something may need to be addressed!

8. Did you do anything as a result of what you felt or discovered after you thought about God breathing on you? Perhaps that day you did or even later in the journey.

I invite you to have fun with this. You don't have to answer each question, just see if one of the questions (or more) is relevant to what happened when you felt the wind hit you. Look forward in joy as you embark with this wonderful intention to know God better on a personal basis. It will have rich rewards for you.

In closing I ask once more that you leave your thoughts in the form of a review to let others know your experience. If you're comfortable sharing what experience you had, or greater relationship occurred, let others know! It will be your way of helping others grow closer to Him as well.

May your journey blow you away!

Ricky

Other Books by Ricky Manna:

The Art of Surrender

Quotes and Power Phrases That Matter

Before You Consider Suicide - Read This..

Bible Verses That Will Rock Your Sandals

Original Sin - What it is & How It Affects Your Life Today

Acknowledgements

I wish to thank all the people, pastors, authors and leaders who have opened my eyes to the truth of this reality thereby preparing me for the next one.

Thank you!

Ricky Manna

Made in the USA
Columbia, SC
02 August 2017